# Garfield
## GETS A LIFE

BY: JIM DAVIS

**BALLANTINE BOOKS • NEW YORK**

TOING
I TOING

MORNING, ODIE

MORNING, ODIE

BARK

THERE YOU GO, BOY

IT SAYS HERE, A SINGLES CLUB IS JUST THE TICKET

...FOR A HAPPENIN' GUY LIKE ME

HEY, BUDDY... DISCO IS DEAD

WHAT?

WHEN?

SIGH

BOY, YOU LEARN A DANCE THEN ZANGO! FOURTEEN YEARS LATER THEY CHANGE IT

GO FIGURE

MAYBE I OUGHTA JUST FORGET ABOUT MEETING ANYONE...EVER. MAYBE I'LL BECOME A NUN

AS LONG AS IT GETS YOU OUT OF THE HOUSE

HI THERE

TAKE A HIKE

NO THANKS, I JUST TOOK ONE

STRIKE TWO

WHAT IS IT, GARFIELD? IS IT MY BREATH? MY LOOKS? MY PERSONALITY?

WHY CAN'T I...

YO THERE!

BUZZ OFF

BUZZ

OOH, STRIKE THREE. YOU'RE OUTTA HERE, BIG GUY

AND NOW, THIS WORD FROM OUR SPONSOR

FRIENDS...

ARE YOU LONELY?

BORED? A LOSER? IS YOUR IDEA OF A FUN SATURDAY NIGHT SITTING AT HOME WATCHING TV

...WITH YOUR CAT?

PPPTTT!

ARE YOU SO BORING THAT YOU COULD MAKE CHEESE YAWN?

ARE YOU SO OUT OF TOUCH THAT YOU THINK DISCO IS STILL "IN"?

HAVE YOU EVER PASSED THE TIME BY COUNTING CEILING TILES?

COMPARED TO YOU DOES A SLUG SEEM HYPERACTIVE?

WELL FRIEND, IF THIS IS YOU, CHEER UP! THERE IS HELP FOR YOU AT THE...

I WONDER IF THEY COULD HELP ME?

REMEMBER FRIENDS, OUR MOTTO IS...

"IF YOU CAN GET A PULSE,

...YOU CAN GET A LIFE."

MAYBE THEY'LL TAKE YOU ANYWAY

"HELLO HELLO WELCOME TO LORENZO'S SCHOOL FOR THE PERSONALITY IMPAIRED." MAY I HELP YOU?

UH, YES, I'M HERE TO GET A LIFE

UH, I MEAN I HAVE A LIFE, BUT IT'S BORING

WELL, IT'S NOT THAT IT'S BORING SO MUCH

YES, I SEE. WE'LL WANT TO START YOU RIGHT OUT IN ROOM 1A

THAT'S "HOW TO MAKE A GOOD FIRST IMPRESSION." DOWN THE HALL, FIRST DOOR ON THE RIGHT

HAVE A NICE LIFE

I'D SETTLE FOR A NICE LUNCH

HOW DO YOU DO? MY NAME IS LORENZO

WHAT IS YOUR NAME?

JON, JON ARBUCKLE

AND THIS IS MY...ER...ARE YOU THE LORENZO IN THE COMMERCIAL?

IN PERSON

GEE, ON T.V. YOU SOUNDED SO... SO...

SO WHAT?

SO ALIVE

OH, THAT WAS A LIP SYNC. YOU KNOW, MY BODY, CHARLTON HESTON'S VOICE

I SEE

ONWARD AND UPWARD, SHALL WE? HAVE A SEAT, MR. ARBUCKLE

NOW, HOW MIGHT I DO THAT? YOU MIGHT ASK

YOU DO THAT BY WALKING RIGHT UP TO THEM...

LOOK THEM RIGHT IN THE...

EYE...

GIVING THEM A FIRM HANDSHAKE...

...AND SAYING, "HELLO, MY NAME IS SO AND SO." EVERYONE TURN TO THE PERSON NEXT TO YOU AND GIVE IT A TRY

HELLO, MY NAME IS...

HELLO, MY NAME IS...

HELLO, MY NAME IS...

HELLO, MY NAME IS...

HELLO, MY NAME IS...

HELLO, MY NAME IS...

HELLO, MY NAME IS JON

HI, MY NAME IS MONA

HELLO, MY NAME IS GARFIELD. YOU'VE PROBABLY NOTICED...

NOTHING IMPRESSES PEOPLE MORE THAN WHEN YOU SPEAK IN A FOREIGN LANGUAGE

BUT YOU DON'T REALLY HAVE TO LEARN A LANGUAGE...

IF YOU CAN SOUND LIKE YOU SPEAK IT

PEOPLE ARE REALLY IMPRESSED IF YOU CAN SPEAK FRENCH OR IF YOU CAN SOUND FRENCH

FOR EXAMPLE, "JE PARLE EN FRANCAIS"

OOOOHHHH!

LE IMPRESSIVE, NO?

YOU KNOW, I'VE HAD JUST ABOUT ENOUGH SOPHISTICATION FOR ONE DAY. HOW 'BOUT YOU?

OUI, MON AMI

HEY, YOU, MONSIEUR DUMB GUY, REMEMBER ME? WHAT AM I? CHOPPED LIVER? DUCK PATÉ? LIVERWURST? BOY, AM I HUNGRY

IT'S BEEN A WONDERFUL DAY, JON. CLASS WAS GREAT AND DINNER WAS FUN

BUT MOST OF ALL I'VE REALLY ENJOYED TALKING TO YOU

UNTIL I MET YOU, I THOUGHT I WAS THE ONLY PERSON IN THE WORLD TO GET MY TONGUE CAUGHT IN AN ELEVATOR DOOR

I'VE REALLY ENJOYED TALKING TO YOU TOO, MONA, AND WE DIDN'T HAVE TO SPEAK FRENCH

WHAT?

THINK ABOUT IT

WE HAD A WONDERFUL EVENING WITHOUT HAVING TO RELY ON ANYTHING WE LEARNED IN CLASS TODAY

PHEW!

OH NO! POOR JON! HE DOESN'T KNOW WHAT HE'S GETTING INTO. I MUST STOP HIM BEFORE HE MULTIPLIES!

THEN IN MY SENIOR YEAR...WHA?!!

GARFIELD?! WHAT ARE YOU DOING?

JON, YOU DON'T KNOW WHAT YOU'RE DOING

WHAT A SWEET CAT

DON'T LISTEN TO HER, JON! SHE'S TRYING TO GET TO YOU THROUGH ME!

WOULD YOU LIKE ME TO SCRATCH BEHIND YOUR EARS?

OH! THAT'S GOOD

SHE'S VERY GOOD, JON. ONCE SHE HAS ME IN HER CLUTCHES SHE'LL...

PERHAPS JUST A LITTLE BIT BEHIND THIS EAR

JON, LISTEN CAREFULLY. THIS IS ALL A...

JUST A LITTLE LOWER, PLEASE... THIS IS ALL A SINISTER PLOT TO GET YOU TO...OH YES! NOW...

ACHOOO!

OH...EXCUSE ME

ARE YOU OKAY?

I'M FINE, REALLY. IT'S JUST THAT I'M... THAT I'M...

ACHOO!

ALLERGIC TO CACHOO!

OH, FOR A MINUTE THERE I THOUGHT YOU SAID YOU WERE ALLERGIC TO CATS!

I... I AM... ACHOO!

OH, NO!

AW, TOO BAD. WHAT A SHAME. SHE WAS SO CUTE. AND SUCH A GOOD EAR SCRATCHER, TOO

COME ALONG, JON

SAY GOODBYE TO YOUR LITTLE FRIEND. IT'S TIME TO FIX DINNER, ANYWAY

WELL, WHAT ARE YOU WAITING ON?

THIS IS TERRIBLE

I'M SORRY, JON, SNIFF'

CAN'T YOU TAKE SHOTS FOR YOUR ALLERGY?

THERE'S SOMETHING TO BE SAID FOR SENIORITY

CAN WE STILL SEE EACH OTHER SOMETIME, JON?

I'D LIKE THAT

NOT WITHOUT A CHAPERON. JON'S MORE THAN A FRIEND TO ME... HE'S MY MEAL TICKET

COME ON. I'LL TAKE YOU HOME

HANG ON! WAIT FOR ME!